THE PSALM OF CHRIST

Also by Chad Walsh

Behold the Glory
Campus Gods on Trial
C.S. Lewis: Apostle to the Skeptics
Doors into Poetry
Early Christians of the 21st Century
Eden Two-Way
The End of Nature
The Factual Dark
Faith and Behavior (with Eric Montizambert)
From Utopia to Nightmare
Garlands for Christmas
God at Large
Hang Me Up My Begging Bowl
The Honey and the Gall
Knock and Enter
The Literary Legacy of C.S. Lewis
Nellie and Her Flying Crocodile
A Rich Feast
The Rough Years
Stop Looking and Listen
Twice Ten (with Eva Walsh)
The Unknowing Dance

The Psalm of Christ

Forty Poems on the Twenty–second Psalm

SECOND EDITION

Chad Walsh

HAROLD SHAW PUBLISHERS
WHEATON, ILLINOIS

Unless otherwise indicated, Scripture quotations
are from the *King James Version*. Selected
quotations from the *Revised Standard Version* (RSV)
and the *Great Bible* of 1539 (GB) are also included.

Cover photo: David Singer

Library of Congress Cataloging in Publication Data

Walsh, Chad, 1914-
  The Psalm of Christ.

  1. Christian poetry, American. 2. Bible. O.T.
Psalms XXII—Meditations. I. Title.
PS3545.A583P7 1982   811'.54   82-5566
ISBN 0-87788-700-4   AACR2

Printed in the United States of America

First Printing, June 1982

For Eva
My Wife

INVOCATION

Great-hearted Christ, importunate and mild,
  Whose time was time enough for woman and well,
Whose arms were slow enough for any child,
  And made the necessary trip to hell,
Fate-parted Christ, why did you leave me so?
  In bread and wine and bed and vine I see you
And in the small gnats when the sun is low
  And in the darkness too. They cannot be you,
Not all can be. Late-started Christ, return;
  Be in a certain time and public place.
If they can see you once, my eyes will learn
  To see you under any other face
You wear, and if all faces are your own
And places, then I worship you alone.

CONTENTS

FOREWORD TO THE SECOND EDITION

This little book has demonstrated a surprising longevity. It was first published in 1963 (Westminster Press, hardcover). After some years it passed out of print, to reappear eventually in paperback, thanks to the same publisher. A few years ago this edition also went out of print. The present edition, which makes the book available for a third time, is the act of faith of Harold Shaw Publishers, who share my hope that these forty poems will continue to speak, religiously and poetically, to the reader who pauses to give them a hearing.

Ordinarily I hesitate to trace the history of my poems. Let the poems speak for themselves, I say inwardly. But the genesis of *The Psalm of Christ* is indirect and perhaps of some interest in itself. It may even demonstrate one way in which Bible and poet can enrich each other. To explain this, let me set down briefly how the poems came into existence.

Many years ago, when I finally started reading the gospels systematically, I came to the outcry of Jesus at the ninth hour: "*Eli, Eli, lama sabachthani?*"—"My God, my God, why hast thou forsaken me?"

What did Jesus' outcry mean? Could it be that at the last

hour his sense of God's presence vanished like a bright mirage? Could it be—still darker possibility—that the presence had been a mirage all along, and that only the agony of the crucifixion taught Jesus to abandon an illusion? Was it possible that in the dying moment of agonized life he saw the world as it actually is, void of God, an empty thing of random events and tortured nerves?

That cry has pierced through the centuries; I was merely late in hearing it. But once I did hear it, it haunted me. Only much later (around 1960) I learned what I should already have known—that the words are, verbatim, the beginning of the Twenty-second Psalm. I then turned to that psalm to see whether it would throw any light on the cry.

The psalm begins with a sense of desolation, developed through verse after verse in language of utter desperation, and then (in verse 22), without any transition at all, turns into a triumphant thanksgiving for deliverance and a proclamation of God's victory.

In the light of the psalm, Jesus may have been doing two things. In his cry he confessed a real sense of deprivation. Enduring whatever any man can be called upon to endure, he endured even the withdrawal of God's perceived presence. The opening words of the psalm served him for an utterance of complete forsakenness. But, good Jew that he was, he had learned the psalms by heart. He knew how the Twenty-second Psalm ends. Perhaps he was reciting the whole psalm, not simply to express his agony of loneliness, but also to comfort himself with the hope and conviction that God the Father, though now invisible to the eyes of his spirit, was none the less with him, and that God is always victorious in the end.

My understanding of the psalm was nothing novel. Since Jesus himself repeated at least the opening words on the cross, he must in some way have identified himself with the nameless sufferer of the psalm. His enemies also, though mockingly, associated the psalm with him. Looking up at the cross they taunted him: "He saved others; himself he cannot save. If he be the King of Israel, let him now come down from the cross, and we will believe him. *He trusted in God; let him deliver him* now, if he will have him: for he said, I am the Son of God." The italicized words are from the Twenty-second Psalm.

Certainly the disciples regarded the Twenty-second Psalm as peculiarly "the psalm of Christ." John explicitly quotes it: "Then the soldiers, when they had crucified Jesus, took his garments, and made four parts, to every soldier a part; and also his coat: now the coat was without seam, woven from the top throughout. They said therefore among themselves, Let us not rend it, but cast lots for it, whose it shall be: that the Scripture might be fulfilled, which saith, *They parted my raiment among them, and for my vesture they did cast lots.*" There are similar echoes in the synoptic gospels.

Finally, the young church appropriated the psalm and made it Christ's. The Letter to the Hebrews says: "For both he that sanctifieth and they who are sanctified are all of one: for which cause he is not ashamed to call them brethren, saying, *I will declare thy name unto my brethren, in the midst of the church will I sing praise unto thee.*"

I learned these things. Meanwhile, I found myself writing poems now and then, suggested by individual verses or phrases from the psalm. Sometimes I was trying to understand the psalm in the light of Christ, and sometimes to understand Christ in the light of the psalm. Always, I suppose, I was trying to understand myself in the light of both.

After I had finished a dozen or so poems, the psalm still held me. I decided to go on until I had forty poems. One has to call a halt somewhere, and it occurred to me that an occasional person might wish to use the poems for Lenten reading. I must, however, interject a warning at this point. The order of the poems is determined by the psalm and not by the special days of Lent. Unless this is borne in mind, the reader will be dumfounded to discover that his Good Friday meditation is a poem about my four daughters indulging in a water fight!

These forty poems were written over a period of three or four years, and reflect many changing moods as well as a good deal of technical experimentation in the verse forms. As the series gradually took form, I realized that a few slightly earlier poems, viewed retrospectively, belonged in *The Psalm of Christ,* and I incorporated them at the appropriate places.

Pious poetry deserves no special favors. A poem is a poem, and it is the poet's job to write the best poems he can, regardless of his subject. This is a book of poems, and they must stand as poems. Indeed, I dare hope that they will be poetically meaningful even to the person who does not literally share the particular faith that underlies them.

One word more. There is a special section of notes at the back of the book for anyone who wishes an explanation of certain poems or of the way I used particular phrases from the psalm.

Chad Walsh
(1982)

ACKNOWLEDGMENTS

Grateful acknowledgment is made to the following periodicals, in which many of these poems first appeared:

The Christian Century (poems 10, 22, 23, 27, 30)
Colorado Quarterly (26)
Epoch (32)
ETS Journal (21, 24, 25, 37)
Ladies' Home Journal (13)
Living Church (1, 11, 30, 34)
The New York Times (38). Reprinted by permission.
Outposts (33)
Prairie Schooner (Invocation)
Presbyterian Life (2)
Spirit: A Magazine of Poetry (3, 29, 39). Copyrighted by The Catholic Poetry Society of America.
Time of Singing (35)
Voices (36)

Two eminent Biblical scholars—Prof. Abraham J. Heschel, of The Jewish Theological Seminary of America, and Prof. Harvey H. Guthrie, Jr., of Episcopal Theological Seminary —read the manuscript of this book and made many valuable suggestions. They are not responsible for any deficiencies that remain, but the book is a better one for their kind cooperation. I also wish to offer my deepest thanks to my good friend the Rev. Edward T. Dell, Jr., who encouraged me all along the way and also performed that ultimate office of friendship—helping me read the proofs.

1 *My God, my God, look upon me* (Verse 1, GB).

And God looked down at God that day,
And God looked up and tried to pray.

He prayed to nothing he could see.
"Father," he said, "look down at me."

It was the strangest of his days.
He could not see the Father's gaze.

He could not hear the Father speak.
He felt his own lips growing weak.

He saw the brightness drain from sky.
He saw the noon darken and die.

He saw the soldiers playing dice.
He told a thief of Paradise.

He gave a mother to a son.
He knew and said the day was done.

He drank the darkness, and he said,
"Into thy hands," and he was dead.

2

Why hast thou forsaken me? (Verse 1).

Perhaps the Socrates he had never read,
The Socrates that Socrates poorly understood,
Had the answer. From opposites, opposites
Are generated. Cold to heat, heat to cold,
Life to death, and death to life. Perhaps the grave's
Obscenity is the womb, the only one
For the glorified body. It may be
Darkness alone, darkness, black and mute,
Void of God and a human smile, filled
With hateful laughter, dirty jokes, rattling dice,
Can empty the living room of all color
So that the chromatic slide of salvation
Fully possesses the bright screen of vision.

Or perhaps, being man, it was simply
He must first go wherever man had been,
To whatever caves of loneliness, whatever
Caverns of no light, deep damp darkness,
Dripping walls of the spirit, man has known.

I have called to God and heard no answer,
I have seen the thick curtain drop, and sunlight die;
My voice has echoed back, a foolish voice,
The prayer restored intact to its silly source.
I have walked in darkness, he hung in it.
In all of my mines of night, he was there first;
In whatever dead tunnel I am lost, he finds me.
My God, my God, why hast thou forsaken me?
From his perfect darkness a voice says, I have not.

3 *O my God, I cry in the daytime, but thou hearest not* (Verse 2).

O thou who hast no nerves and canst not feel
Electric pulsings of the ache of time,
Pure spirit thou, from no beginning day,
And moving to no end nor transformation,
    Eternally and now,

To whom the blazing birth of galaxies
Is yesterday and the morning of tomorrow,
Who in a long thought beholdest the slime
Of latent life take fins and legs and wings
    And cathedrals rise,

Before whose eyes of undivided spirit
The ice-seas ebb and flow, and the slow planet
Obeys the yearly treadmill of its course,
Obscurely making for its destined portion
    Of final ice or fire,

Thou in the leisure of eternity,
Have pity on thy little things of time
In whom the beating heart's a ticking clock
And every leaf evicted to the ground
    An almanac of death.

Be what we are, be born, be young, and die,
And wrap the traitor torture of the nerves
In the cool circles of the robot globe.
If thou canst not, then leave and give us leave
    To curse God and die.

4

O my God, I cry in the daytime, but thou hearest not; and in the night season, and am not silent (Verse 2).

When darkness covered Job against his bed
It almost covered memories of the dead.

The wind that swept his children to their death
Receded to a faintly stirring breath.

The silence canceled out the oral proof
That they lay flat beneath a flattened roof.

Knowing that God is good and God is might,
He drank and drained the stillness of the night.

He willed a deepening vagueness of the mind
And almost knew again that God is kind.

In the instant that total darkness came
He willed and blessed and spoke the holy name.

He woke, a ball of pus from sole to crown.
He found a pile of ashes and sat down.

He scraped his skin with slivers of a pot.
His wife said, "Curse God, die," but he would not.

There was a later day of whirling wind.
God never said which of the two had sinned.

So Job repented of he knew not what,
And what was not forgiven was forgot.

5   *Thou art holy, O thou that inhabitest the praises of Israel* (Verse 3).

Not height nor breadth nor length is separation,
For holiness construes its own dimension.
The time-warp of the soul lends apprehension
Of who is in each prayer and no nation.

Continually the cherubim and seraphim
Revolve in hierophantic stances
And shape their cries to the ecstatic dances
Of those whose eyes drink plenitude of him.

The elders cannot keep their crowns for joy;
Holy, who was, and is, and is to come,
He sits upon the throne, and Abraham
Skates on the crystal sea, at last a boy.

6 *Our fathers hoped in thee; they trusted in thee, and thou didst deliver them* (Verse 4, GB).

Come stand with me on this other side.
If we can stand, we have not died.

Our faith was wilder than his deed.
His act was equal to our need.

The chariots came, a while they floated;
Horses and men are vague and bloated.

In sluggish tide they ebb and flow.
Though we have many miles to go,

And desert miles, before we see
A vineyard grape or olive tree,

Though bones will bleach in wilderness
For forty years, yet let us bless

The Lord who triumphed gloriously
And laid our dry road through the sea,

And will lead the years until we stand,
Some of us, in the promised land.

7

They cried unto thee, and were delivered: they trusted in thee, and were not confounded (Verse 5).

Ago as Berlin and the airlift, I,
Between both blues at sea—
Curried and brushed clean by the salt of wind—
Decided not to lie,
And Father, I have sinned
Against you and that sky,
Against the perfect sea.
Now put some truth in me.

O put some truth in me against the day I die.
The thickets of my faith are whipped of leaves and
     thinned.
Their branches break in any devil's wind.

Feed me with truth, wheaten brown and blood-
     dripping.
There, I am filled, belly and coursing vein.
I will not tell a lie;
I will not say disease and death and pain
Part like the Red Sea at a whiff of Christian prayer
To let the fleeing pilgrim through, nor say
The fever-feebled brain
Will lose the torpid stare,
Nor arms, brain parted, ever move again.
I say, the hangman jokes the way to work
And sleeps like you and me at close of day.
Your naked back cannot
For all your faith untie one bloody knot
To smooth the jailer's scourge. And cancer kills.
Love lies upon the rack,
Love fouls into divorce,
And miracles are best a random lot.
Though God is here and there and everywhere

He seldom runs to save
From justice, sudden death, and falling hair
The faithful in the chapel of their prayer.

And yet he saves. The silence tells me so.
He saves through Jesus, whom he did not save,
Through Jesus, nailed up like a naughty slave.
How can this be? The nails and crossbeam speak
Words to a kind of ear. The rattling tongue
Ceases. I do not know
The words of answer to this alien voice.
I cannot tell you what he saves me from
Or for. For there he hung
And hangs, and we have made a tacit choice.
Utter and silent Savior, I rejoice.

8

But as for me, I am a worm, and no man; a very scorn of men, and the outcast of the people (Verse 6, GB).

Cereal boxes and empty cans,
Corpses of dogs, and fleshless bones,
Chromium and rust of broken cars,
Shards of shattered bricks and stones

Be his garden, the last he will see,
A vertical beam for an olive tree.

Fires that Adam and Cain first lighted
Dully consume the shattered denials.
Here the rejected things of the earth
Come to the last of public trials.

Nailed to the sky in low relief
Thief and a God, God and his thief.

Hammer in hand, nails in my pocket
Here at the foot of the cross I stand.
Blood on the hammer, blood on my fingers.
Jesus, more blood, to dry my hand.

9

But as for me, I am a worm, and no man; a very scorn of men, and the outcast of the people (Verse 6, GB).

We hung Jesus Christ on a sour apple tree
And left him there for the good folk to see.

10

All they that see me laugh me to scorn (Verse 7).

The seventh day he rested and he laughed.
The job was done, it was a job well done.
Heaven's blue arch was set above the earth.
Dry land and water kept their separate bounds.
Green things, in ecstasy of seed and pollen,
Marched upland with their flags of frond and leaf.
An ardent sun and bashful moon repelled
The darkness always waiting for a chance.
Whales and minnows swam in a glitter of water,
Bear lumbered off with bear, fox played with fox,
And Adam looked at Eve, and felt his soul
Dissolving in the friendship of her eyes.
And God looked down, and it was very good.
And God looked down, and laughed. He laughed
    for joy.

And Adam, you laughed too; you laughed to see
A rib that you could spare grown glorious
In friendly flash of glowing flesh and softly
Shaped breasts. You were a god asleep. The work
Of your slow sleep was good. Helpmeet and wife,
A kind of little sister, bone of your bones,
She stood before you in that first perfection.
You laughed, she laughed, God laughed. Laughter
    was good.

Why did you let her eat that silly fruit?
Or if she ate it while your back was turned,
You were the elder by a day at least
And did not need to follow her example.
Perhaps—for God is good—you could have
    spanked
And kissed her quickly back to innocence
Before the taste of evil set on edge

Her teeth, your teeth, the teeth of embryos.
You could have tried. You ate. Cain whets his
   knife.

And Jesus writhes upon the poisoned tree.
The passers laugh. God's darkness keeps its silence.

11

All they that see me laugh me to scorn: they shoot out the lip, they shake the head, saying, He trusted on the Lord that he would deliver him: let him deliver him, seeing he delighted in him (Verses 7–8).

"Show us a miracle," we said.
The double pair of nail-holes bled.
The rose of thorn-pricks ringed his head.

"Show us a miracle," we pleaded,
And almost feared. Suppose God heeded
Our giggling plea, and interceded?

The ninth hour came. No God appeared.
He hung there limp and neatly speared.
Why should a helpless God be feared?

12 *Thou art he that took me out of the womb* (Verse 9).

I will sing a new song unto the Lord.
His glory has not worthily been spoken
Though every leafy tree and blade of grass
Whispers in wind to tell his hidden Name
And though the chipmunk, charged with sun and
    air,
Descends into his temple under earth

To say his prayers of praise. O choirs of earth—
Leaf, scale, feather, fur, hair—proclaim the Lord!
Set in movement the molecules of air.
Let the secret word openly be spoken,
Let the high echoes answer back the Name,
And breath of angels furrow through the grass.

Though he has made me fleeting as the grass,
Though mole and I are shaped of brother earth
And to the earth return—O praise his Name,
All things that breed and die. Know he is Lord
Of the amino acids, and the word spoken
To dust raised Adam's eyes into the air.

For thou hast lifted me into the air
A little while, to tread the patient grass
With moving weight, and hear thy word spoken—
Eden, Sinai, the ends of any earth,
The cross into the skull. Speak the word, Lord,
The private word into my heart: thy Name.

O speak it now, and speak my hidden name
Planted in thee before birds broke the air.
Say who I am and introduce my Lord.
Ye little lives that nestle in the grass,

Slim creatures underground, wings above earth,
Be silent quickly, for the Lord has spoken.

Be clamorous quickly, for the Lord has spoken.
Sing in polyphony his public Name,
Descended out of heaven to the earth.
Say, sing, chant the Name of Jesus in air
Kissing with Easter green the risen grass
That is the emerald carpet of the Lord.

The risen Lord has looked at me and spoken.
Though I am grass, he calls me by a name.
Sing high, bright air; praise him, brothers of earth.

13 *Thou didst make me hope when I was upon my mother's breasts* (Verse 9).

Why are your eyes so far away,
  Little one, little one?
What are your lips shaped to say,
  My son, my son?

A breast for your lips and milk for your need,
  I offer my little one.
But where do your eyes steadily feed,
  Jesus, my little son?

The sun in the sky, a fleece of a cloud,
  I see, and my little one,
And a lark sings soft, and my heart sings loud
  To carol a newborn son.

Take what I have, the milk and the breast,
  Close your eyes, little one.
See when you must, but sleep is best,
  This hour, Jesus my son.

14
Thou didst make me hope when I was upon my mother's breasts. I was cast upon thee from the womb (Verses 9–10).

Since it was always, there was no surprise
   To see the light
Come calm into my open or shut eyes
   By day or night.
   I had no time of wonder nor of fright.

I thought it was my mother's breasts that shone,
   But then night fell,
And then her breasts, save taste and touch, were
     gone.
   I could not tell
   How light could hide her breasts, but all was
     well.

I thought it was my brothers all aglow
   Or Joseph's saw,
And when I learned to read, it seemed to flow
   From Moses' law,
   But then it glimmered from a fox's paw.

But when I climbed the mountain with the three
   And brightness played
From face to face, leaf to leaf, tree to tree,
   And Simon said,
   "The light," and knelt to me, I was afraid.

15 *There is none to help* (Verse 11).

Said active priest, "My work has increased
   Until I'm weary and dizzy.
But write his name down; when next I'm in
     town . . .
   Today I'm frightfully busy."

Samaritan said, "He's so close to dead,
   It's immoral to waste my resources.
There's a road I must go, where three men in a row
   Were beaten and robbed of their horses."

Said Roman guard, "Don't take it so hard;
   It won't last long in this sun."
He rattled the dice; he thought once or twice,
   "I wonder if God has a son."

16 *They gape upon me with their mouths* (Verse 13, GB).

Bright butterfly, pinned to the wooden wall
Of history, we were your juvenile
Delinquents, dead-end kids, fresh from the brawl
Of usual gangs, the switchblade, the mean smile.
We had you where we wanted you a while,
And while you wriggled there, love of a kind
Rustled among our backslaps, to reconcile
Our rival gangs, effectively combined
To keep you there. It ended. They took you down.
We started home, each in his surly cluster,
To the dark streets, with broken bottles and bluster
To hold our turf and vested territory
Against the kids from other parts of town.
And that's the end of our part in the story.

17 *My strength is dried up like a potsherd* (Verse 15).

My eyes can see my cancerous skin,
Your X-ray eyes can look within
And mark the cancer of my guts.
Lord have mercy upon me.

Oh, skin can hide the eaten gut
And wool can clothe the sprawling smut,
But in your eyes I always see—
Christ have mercy upon me.

Behind the smile I daily wear
There smirks in red and hollow stare
The eyes and teeth of Halloween,
The idiot's fossil grimace.

What if the eyes that see could cure?
Could burn the filth and leave me pure?
They say you died because of me.
Jesus, see, brand me, and heal.

18 *Many dogs are come about me* (Verse 16, GB).

Caiaphas was a Siamese cat,
　　Twitching nose and eyes of ice;
He stalked the troublesome Nazarene rat
　　For a Paschal sacrifice.

He led a pack of baying hounds
　　To see the Procurator.
The great elk trembled at the sounds
　　And ordered a basin of water.

The curs of the city came fresh on the trail.
　　"Caesar," they barked, and louder still,
"Barabbas!" Caiaphas twitched his tail,
　　And "Jesus," he mewed, and "kill."

The hounds took up the feline cry,
　　Passed it along to the yelping pack.
Pilate said with a sigh, "Then let him die,"
　　Dabbled in water, turned his back.

The curs ran off to the Place of the Skull,
　　Barked at the foot of the cross.
They never knew—for their wits were dull—
　　A Siamese cat had been their boss.

19 *The assembly of the wicked have inclosed me* (Verse 16).

You have the advantage, sir, two thousand years,
To put it roundly, and your obsessive fears
Are not the same as mine were. You can be
Expedient when you will and absolute with me.
But time at least dissolves the politic lies
With which we dust the public's bleary eyes,
And I can speak as one man to another.
I am, whether you know it or not, your brother.
To see him dead we used the classic tools—
False witnesses and bribes and noisy fools.
The charge was immaterial. In fact,
Whatever would lead the Governor to act,
Or rather not to act, was all we needed.
We faltered for a time, but we succeeded.
But you perhaps are more concerned with why.
Better that one man, than a nation, die.
God's not exempt from *Realpolitik*.
Messiahs are the opiate of the weak.
We saved the nation from the ruinous meek.
I've met you honestly upon this case.
Imagine that you stood there in my place.
Is there one man you would not crucify
Lest your nation and nation's God should die?

20 *They pierced my hands and my feet: I may tell all my bones* (Verse 17 GB).

There was a man of Galilee
  Hey ho hey ho
There was a man of Galilee
And he could walk upon the sea
  I'll be true to my love
If my love be true to me.

The priests and elders came they came
  Hey ho hey ho
The priests and elders came they came
They carried torches all aflame
  "I'll kiss him" the little man said
And Judas was his name.

They took him off to the courthouse room
  Hey ho hey ho
They took him off to the courthouse room
And stood him up to meet his doom
  Caiaphas, wink at the elders
I'll give you a lily in bloom.

Pontius Pilate he washed his hands
  Hey ho hey ho
Pontius Pilate he washed his hands
He told the people "There he stands"
  "Kill him" the people screamed
And Pilate gave commands.

They took the man of Galilee
  Hey ho hey ho
They took the man of Galilee
And nailed him up on a crooked tree
  I'll be true to my love
My love was true to me.

21

They part my garments among them, and cast lots upon my vesture (Verse 18).

I threw a seven, so the coat was mine.
It smelled of cornfields, hay, a touch of lily,
And sweat. There was a spot or two of blood
But that would wash out. All in all, I thought,
Not a bad bonus for a day's dull work.
I'd trade it to some Jew at the bazaar,
Ought to be worth a jug or two of wine
At going rates.

        Somehow, I wonder, I never
Got around to it. Carried the silly thing
Stuck in my blanket roll, all the way here
To Gaul. Never sold it. Never wore it.
Was mustered out and settled here in Gaul
On this little farm that Caesar gave me.
Married a native girl. Not bad. Needed
A bit of training, but the tip of the whip
Taught her some Latin and company manners.
Not bad at all. There she is now at the oven.
Yes, that's the coat. A little long for her.
Likes it, she says. Keeps her warm these cold days.
Have supper with us? A face fresh out of Rome
And a good Roman tongue are luxuries here.
Fine, glad you can stay. She'll set an extra place.

The man? The Jew who wore the coat? Oh, he—
You know the Jews, they hate us foreigners
But hate each other more. Quarreling crew.
Was glad when I was reassigned to Gaul.
They did him in, and Pilate let them do it.
What was his name? He was a quiet one there,
Not like that thief that bawled and damned my
     eyes.

What was his name? It was so long ago.
He's buried, he'll stay buried. When a man is dead
What does a name matter? Time for supper.
It isn't Roman wine, but let's drink to Caesar.

22

Be not thou far from me, O Lord (Verse 19).

I cannot gain again their innocence
And ignorance. I cannot see a cloud
Less than an airplane's height above the earth
And say, "We saw him disappear behind it;
Soon he'll return and bring a shining crowd

Of angels." No, the rocket and the sputnik,
Mount Palomar, inquire and do not find it,
That face, one face. If it is hid in space,
It is so many galaxies away
No instrument has seen and countersigned it.

If he is farther, he's no good to me.
Then I must find him anywhere I pray
And closer than the lashes of my eyes
And surer than my red heart at its beating
And wilder than a tiger on its prey,

And he must have me for his Eucharist,
Digest my solitude by simple eating.
I am not whole until you take me whole,
Nor free until I scatter in your cells,
Nor saved, save lost past cheating and entreating.

23 *Deliver . . . my darling from the power of the dog* (Verse 20).

I see you playing with the neighbor's dog,
A little brother for a littlest daughter.
You throw a broken bough into the lake
And he retrieves it with a swirl of paws.

In him a birthright cunning of the water
Excels the learning of your timid strokes.
He lives and moves and has his being by laws
Surer and kinder than any you will know.

Although he moves, his kinsmen are the oaks
With taproots grazing in the thoughtless earth.
His motives grow beneath the surface snow
Of measured duty and the intellect.

He knows of death as little as you of birth;
He is not damned nor purchased for salvation;
He is not called to take it or reject;
His flailing paws dumbly confess his God.

Do not be led by him. The dark negation
Of reason and the facile loss of sin
Are not for you. An image stamps you odd,
And when God calls, you must go oddly in.

24

Save me from the lion's mouth; thou hast heard me also from among the horns of the unicorns (Verse 21, GB).

The lion's breath is bad,
  It smells of bloody meat.
I should be very sad
  If he chose me to eat.

Ever and then he trails me
  And takes a bite or two,
But Jesus never fails me,
  He plunges into view,

Drives the monster from my nose
  With flick of knotted whip.
I run to count my toes
  And medicate my hip.

So thanks to him, I'm almost whole.
  No common lion can faze him.
The lion tamer saves my soul.
  My lips, though nipped, will praise him.

But unicorn so pure
  With eyes of liquid soul
And horn so straight and sure—
  Don't let him leave a hole

Where once a heart was. Don't
  Let all my blood be spilled.
I trust that Jesus won't.
  He doesn't want me killed.

My heart and blood belong
  To him who owns my soul.

He makes my trinity strong
    And he will save me whole.

When I am pure and know
    I am, he teaches me
To pray, as long ago,
    He taught in Galilee:

   Forgive us our virtues
   As we forgive those who are virtuous against
      us.

25

I will declare thy name unto my brethren: in the midst of the congregation will I praise thee (Verse 22).

Dearly beloved, Moses gave you tablets
Of stone, a pair, on which to read, engraved,
The Tetragrammaton's ten fingers pointing
To freedom for the recently enslaved.

I give you Greek for Hebrew, fish for stone,
The Pentagrammaton for the unspoken
Four letters of the Name. Behold the fish.
The tablets and the Temple screen are broken.

I speak the name without deceit: ΙΧΘΥΣ.
First the iota, ΙΗΣΟΥΣ—*Yahweh saves.*
Then chi, ΧΡΙΣΤΟΣ, *anointed one, Messiah,*
Expert of God from crib to emptied graves.

Next theta upsilon, ΘΕΟΣΥΙΟΣ,
The Son of God, no simple prophet this.
And sigma last, ΣΩΤΗΡ, *savior,* who took
The handshake of the nails and Judas' kiss.

From the primal ocean of that first love
Before a mammal scampered up a tree
The fish of your redemption climbed ashore
And breathed, saying, "Eat me and swim with me."

26 *Ye that fear the Lord, praise him* (Verse 23).

The honeysuckle raped me by the fence.
O thou, the perfume of the Northern Lights,
Whose worm disturbs and frees the impacted roots,
The ice was ready with a numbing sense
And all the while the mockingbird imputes
The answer of the apples to my tongue.
The rain descends in regimental flights
And once the grief of Orpheus was sung
In such a night. Wherever he may be
He's not a breathing body's length from me
With all the planets and the stars to save
And constant inventory still to make
Of every whited sepulcher and grave
Against the fury of the newer stars
And when the tidal waves suspend and break,
The time-forsaken fish gasp into breathing
To flow above the landing of a lake.
Good friend, forbear, forbear for Jesus' sake,
The love that stamps itself in purple scars,
It is the night has faultlessly undone me,
The darkness of this nakedness and the teething,
My God, my God, look not so hungrily upon me.

27

*He hath not despised nor abhorred the affliction
of the afflicted; neither hath he hid his face from him; but
when he cried unto him, he heard* (Verse 24).

Brother spirit, brother of mine and kin,
Not from one womb but from one hand descending
At the direct will of the common maker
With no message of the flesh giving the word
Incarnation; you who with me unending

Praises sing to the One whom we behold
Naked of the shielding senses, who heard
The primal praises singing in his ear
Before he planted angels in his sky
Or built a planet and a singing bird;

You whom no midnight rapids of the dark
Conduit impelled to meeting, and to lie
In the expansive night, swelling in sweetness,
Nirvana of the nine moons, laid in deep
Consent—you never born and not to die—

My brother. Not for us the measured ration
Of golden leaf fall, green return to keep
The checklist of the seasons used and done,
And make of every thicket dull with frost
The skulls and crossbones of a charnel heap,

And not in us the sovereign power to take
The firm, ambiguous flesh. Never and lost
Is it to us. Not God nor beast nor man,
We cannot bargain for a trial descent,
Pledging stigmata to defray the cost.

Holy, holy, holy, you sing with me
For him who shaped us to his plain intent.

We sing, and being in the heavens we fill
The heavens with the record of the Fact
Who authored us for lesser facts. Not meant

For any change are we, for our perfection
Is here and now and ever. No prayer or act
Can lift us higher. We flap our wings in heaven.
And any change in altitude must be
Nearer the brown flames where too closely packed

For flight our rebel brothers of the dawn
Lie burning. Jesus Christ who sings with me
Died on a cross but not for us, my brother.
Sinless, we cannot draw from an atonement.
We own no chains. He cannot set us free.

28
My praise is of thee in the great congregation
(Verse 25, GB).

It is a kind of alchemy.
The sugar bowl, though glass, is turned to silver,
And silver is the small aluminum tray.

The plain oak table, cleared of books
And magazines, and moved before the fireplace,
Is holy now, beneath the holy vessels.

The Dells, the Jacksons, Durhams, Scotts,
And Hockings come in clusters few by few.
There will be many children here to bless.

Outdoors, the lake sings in slow ripples,
And there is singing in the long pine needles.
The old reed organ teaches us to sing.

I speak the bread and body broken.
Those big enough for broken food take, eat.
The blessing hand must feed the little ones.

Why is the room so full? These others,
Who are they? They were and they shall be.
The organ blends their voices with the angels'.

29 *The meek shall eat and be satisfied* (Verse 26).

Her habits followed, more than memories,
That patient morning, and it seemed no strangeness
The hedge of thorn marched white and red beside
    her,
Unbroken hour on hour, hiding and barring
The home that she obscurely knew
Had sent for her.

All hedges open somewhere, said her habits,
Not where one wished them to, but where they did,
With no good reason but the master's will,
Decreed before the building stones were laid;
Open on avenue and mansion
Or barn and cottage.

And so with no surprise and no complaint
She saw at last the narrow wooden gate,
A gray gap in the green and white and red.
Across the top a narrow sign was posted.
She spelled it out and was at ease:
Servants' Entrance.

As one with rights she put her shabby bag
Upon the grass and grasped the heavy bar.
The weathered gate jolted slowly, lifted,
And opened inward with a creaking motion.
She took her bag, entered inside,
And closed the gate.

She hadn't thought that they would meet her there.
Her habits told her that some sort of road
Would lead her to some kind of house, and there,
With habit heightened to an instinct, she
Would know the proper door for her,
And knock and wait.

This time they met her there, inside the gate.
She curtsied, stammering at her mistake,
Certain whoever they had come to meet
Was someone else. With eyes cast down she waited,
Her bag clutched in two hands, ready
To turn and leave.

"Welcome," a voice said. "Let me take your bag."
He spoke her name. A choir of other voices
Lapped at her knees like tides from every shore.
The only word she understood was "glory."
She felt her feet lifting lightly,
And she was singing,

Singing a song her masters had not taught her,
But now she knew it. And at last she looked.
She saw the formal garden of the singers
In full blossom, she saw the manor house,
She saw the one who held her bag
And he was singing.

The voices ceased.
"The table's set,"
He said. "Come in."

30

All the ends of the earth shall remember (Verse 27, RSV).

A tree, a rope, a noose, a knot.
But can I go where he is not?

If ghosts ride seaward, I shall see
His long strides marching on the sea.

In God's black pit there is no rest.
His eyes will part me from the rest.

If ghosts rise upward to the sun,
No shelter shades me from the son.

The sun, the son, the single eye,
And I will be, I will be I.

31

All the ends of the world shall remember and turn unto the Lord: and all the kindreds of the nations shall worship before thee (Verse 27).

The restlessness increased, but so slowly
  (As a dull, throbbing tooth is scarcely noted
  When its voice rises) that my old shoes voted,
And not my brain, to walk the league with folly
East to the east of the ominously holy.

I did not know the vote was cast and numbered,
  I only knew each ten or fifty years
  Drew the Atlantic closer to my ears
While far Wisconsin, close Ohio slumbered,
In growing green, unmanned and unencumbered.

I only knew they joined me one by one,
  The silent others, and we overflowed
  And tramped the bordering fields into a road,
While to the empty west, the rain and sun
Called back the trees and willed young deer to run.

Leaving the emptied continent, we floated
  With the wide current mapped in miles and years
  Past the Azores and through the ancient fears
Of Scylla and Charybdis, and we noted
Crete come and gone. To say that now we floated

Is not the truth. We swam to race the flow
  And sprang dry-footed on the golden sand
  Among the friendly tigers of the land
And ran, still eastward, till we saw aglow
The Town to which all faithful currents flow.

Two thousand tongues and dialects proclaimed
  Praises. And each hand held a building stone.

We raised a House. We did not work alone,
For hidden hands worked faster. And we named
It Beth-El . . . The veil split, the alter flamed,

Brightness raged in the air. When we could see,
    He stood, we stood, our praising tongues stood
        still.
    The walls fell outward at his quiet will.
Earth was a temple from the sea to sea.
"I have a new song," he said. "Sing it with me."

32 *The kingdom is the Lord's* (Verse 28).

Against the setting sun no strategy
Of prayer availed. A smooth predestination
Reddened the sky and dulled it. I could see
Factory panes, first in short conflagration,

And fire depart to trim a little cloud,
Ragged balloon, eastern and high. Soon night
Wrapped the beloved world and equalized
All accidents of decent brown and bright

Frivolity of green. A godly reformation,
Thorough at any rate, to match the drunken
Piety of Cromwell's men, who broke the vision
Of Wells Cathedral to forgotten, sunken

Shards of bright glass beneath the neutral swans
Of the old moat. So the brightness of sun
Or God rides to a night's garroting hands.
It takes a resurrection for a dawn.

33 *The kingdom is the Lord's* (Verse 28).

The stone has rolled away,
  The sun is bright and high
For colts and boys at play.
The stone has rolled away,
Make room for Easter Day.
  There's nothing left to die.
The stone has rolled away.
  The sun is bright and high.

34 *The kingdom is the Lord's* (Verse 28).

The two old women by the mother's bed
Keened into silence and a swaying sleep.
It was not long until the dawn would break.
John, in the other room, was still awake,
Remembering the words her son had said.
At last they slept. At last his sleep was deep.

The mother had not stirred since afternoon;
She lay in the brief peace of those who rest
Between a sickbed and another bed;
A slight breeze brushed the unresponsive head;
The gray hair, faintly in the fading moon,
Stirred white; the rough hands rested on her breast.

The caller did not knock. He stooped and entered;
He did not close the door; he made no sound.
The weary women in their heavy rest
Slept on. He raised his giant hand and blessed
Them with a moment's cross, and then he centered
His slow smile where the sleep was more profound.

Stooping again, as lightly as a child
Takes in his arms a kitten from the floor
He knelt and pressed his heavy arms around
The silent mother, and he made no sound;
He rose as tall as the room would let; he smiled
Downward to her and tiptoed to the door.

The sun was rising as he stepped outside.
His warm arms warded off the morning chill.
The moon was the balloon a playful child
Drops from a top window. The planets filed
In circles all about. From high the guide
Of golden light (not sunlight) reached to fill

The lower blue with gold. Soon all was gold.
The sleeping mother in his arms was set
In gold. "Do you not hear the songs that guide
Us through and to the light?" he asked. She tried
To speak, or so it seemed. She was not old.
Her eyes opened. "Joseph," she said. "Not yet,"

He said, "but soon." She saw and smiled. "I told
Them you would come for me." She closed her
        eyes.
He met her at the singing of the gold.

35

All they that be fat upon earth shall eat and worship (Verse 29).

If there's no love to cast out fear,
Enter with dread, but enter here.

In organ swell and ritual motion,
A rising and a kneeling ocean.

And fingers bless and words are spoken,
And wine is red and bread is broken.

Come with your teeth to crucify him
And spears of lips to taste and try him.

Cannibal teeth feed on his pains
And new blood sing in savage veins.

Unless with Caiaphas you kneel
What God can perish, rise, and heal?

Unless with Caiaphas you die
What God can roof the church with sky?

I saw the ceiling break and fade,
I saw another sun invade.

The hands were gold that held the chalice,
My body was a golden palace.

He made us cannibals. Be bold,
And be the singing of the gold.

36

All they that go down to the dust . . . (Verse 29).

In the old graveyard
The rain and frost
Have done their work.

Names and numbers
Blurred and defaced;
Stones slant and fall.

The hasty sickle
Spares ragged clumps
Of grass by stones.

The old church perished
In fire and smoke
A life ago.

The sheets of paper
To plot the graves
Are ashes too.

Ashes to ashes,
And dust to dust,
Fullness of death.

The old gravedigger
Comes rarely now.
New guests are few.

And in the vagueness
Of scattered stones
He cannot know

Where he is safest,
He and his spade,
From Yorick's skull.

37

All they that go down to the dust shall bow before him (Verse 29).

It was, you might say, a kind of forever
We had waited there, but one must guard
Against an excess of editorial "we"
Which soon rings royal by repetition.
To say it more precisely, some were so new-come
They'd told us how he could measure and drive a
     nail,
A few had heard him preach, and had eaten his
     fish and bread,
And one or two had seen the nailer nailed.

They were the recent ones. The oldest—
They talked of ancient things and faces and acts
But were childish and dull with years and numbers.
     Whenever
The race began, they had been there, from the
     hurricane
That first blew with voices and a command.
They were of those half-apes whose backs
     straightened
And eyes learned to look upward and inward
And whose toes stepped among new damnations
     and loves.

Then there were the ones who belonged between,
Who talked of the light on Moses' face
When he descended the mountain, and who
     smacked their lips
Over the remembered stewpots of Egypt.
Others, the kind that spun questions with no
     answers,
Remembered the Athenian and the beautiful
     gesture

Of a gracious old hand accepting the cup.
Not that these were all. We were a spectrum
From black through brown and red and tan
To the pale pink of the northerners, asking
The road to Valhalla. A passable
But dull time we'd had there. One man,
Gautama, seemed the easiest pleased. He could sit
    for hours
With closed lids, barely breathing, but sometimes,
When the old Athenian dropped by to see him,
You should have heard the two of them talking.

So we lived there, obscurely waiting,
But no one was sure what we waited for,
Or whether it would ever come. Rumors
Were always making the rounds, of course.
Idle men will pass the time somehow.
But it was a tolerable life, and when the thing
    happened—
It was so quiet—there he stood—
A few knew his face, or thought they did—
But said he was changed—like Moses, the light—
When suddenly, quietly he stood there,
It took him a while to get our attention.
New ones were always coming, they could wait.
He stood there. Gradually—it was a funny
    feeling—
Gradually the chatter ceased. We clustered
Around him in circles around circles.
Hardly speaking, we were. We waited.
At last he spoke. It was simple and quiet.
"I must hurry back. There's still work to do—
But first—any of you who want to come along,
I'll drop you off at my father's place,
And meet you there later." He stopped. We waited.
That was all. He raised his arms as a signal

Or blessing, you could hardly say which. Then we
    saw
The hands. Only a few of us understood—
But somehow—well, the memory is confused—
But I do recall Gautama and the old Athenian,
Silent, motionless like cats ready to spring,
But that light in their eyes. They knew him.
They beckoned to Moses and Abraham. The four
Sprang up and led us. *He* led them.
It seemed we hardly did more than round a corner
Before we were there. He left us there.
But he kept his word. In two months, maybe less,
"Hello," he said, and there he was again,
And he raised his arms. The hands shone like the
    face—
But I'm rambling too much—look, there he is,
Where he's been all along. See for yourself.

38 *None can keep alive his own soul* (Verse 29).

Lord, you shall say what it will be this night,
   A pillow or the headsman's block. Decree
   Whatever morning you have willed for me
And it shall be. This body will not fight
For air against the one who made the light
   Take flesh in me. And if it is to be
   This night, level my length as a tall tree
Slants to the brushy earth and sinks from sight.

If it shall be, then be the death complete,
   The body quiet and the soul annulled.
     Bury my name from fame and love and shame
Beneath millennia of insensate feet.
   Let me be deep in death and lulled and dulled
     Until you rouse me with a stranger's name.

39

My seed shall serve him (Verse 31, GB).

Fatherhood is a school of humility, it corrects the
    soul.
Girls are the best school. I have four of them.
Sometimes when I look at them, I wonder where
    I fit in.
I might claim two noses, but their owners wouldn't
    thank me
For the gift. Alison's blond hair is hers, not mine;
When Demie plays the cello I cannot contend my
    poor recorder
Prenatally put music in her. Madeline dances
    ballet,
A straight queen, five foot three. My six feet
    stumble at a fox-trot.
And Sarah-Lindsay, when not shaking the house
    with her declarations,
Does the serene acts of compassion and love with
    the grace
Of a soul that needs no schooling, forethought, or
    prompting.
In short, here they are, and I am glad. But where
    am I in them?

I was most in them at the start. The microscopic
    miracle—
Momentary, essential—was mine four times to
    assist.
It was as though four times I was able to help open
    a door,
And four bright spirits, assorted, entered from
    outer space.

Now they walk the four pilgrim paths, each in her
    style.

What I have told and shown them of God is as
        transient
As the last year I could outswim Sarah in the race
        to the dock.
If they find God, or are found; if they have him,
        or rather
If he has them, it is in four separate and secret
        ways.
Those doors are not mine to open. I do not knock.

Instead let me praise the fact. In any poem I write,
In my handwriting, or the way I build a bookcase
There is more of me than in Demie, Madeline,
Sarah, and Alison. They are a revelation
Not of me, but of the other father. Glory and laud
Forever to him who has given me more than a
        trinity
Of bright messengers, giggling with creation's first
        dawn
In the ballet of a water fight between the float and
        the dock.

40

Proclaim his deliverance to a people yet unborn, that he has wrought it (Verse 31, RSV).

Sleep, sleep the nine months, and enter
The waking world where every moment is a center
Of time's circumference and his
Who was and evermore shall be and is.

Because there was a manger, come
And let the round earth be your blessed home.
Because there was a cross there, cry
For the fall of a broken butterfly.

Because there was an empty tomb
Sing a new song in anybody's room.
Because there was an empty tomb
Kiss any snow and see the roses bloom.

NOTES

The passages in the New Testament that echo the Twenty-second Psalm are as follows:

Verse 1: Matthew 27:46; Mark 15:34

Verses 7–8: Matthew 27:39,43; Mark 15:29; Luke 23:35

Verse 18: Matthew 27:35; Mark 15:24; Luke 23:34; John 19:23–24

Verse 22: Hebrews 2:12

In my quotations from the Twenty-second Psalm I have used the King James Version except where otherwise indicated. Frequently I turned instead to the *Great Bible* of 1539 (GB), long cherished for its liturgical resonance. In a few instances I used the *Revised Standard Version* (RSV). My choice in each case was dictated not by scholarly considerations but by the exigencies of the poem I was writing.

Any Biblical specialist who reads these forty poems will quickly discover that I was not trying to write a learned commentary in verse. I took the psalm pretty much as I found it, without worrying over obscure textual problems. I read it and read it again, thought about it, and meditated on any of the verses that seemed to come alive. I hope that the poems that gradually evolved are, in general, faithful to the spirit of the psalm, as it has been understood by the centuries of Christians pondering it in the light of Christ. But the reader who wishes a technical and exact commentary, and the latest findings of Biblical scholarship, must turn to the scholarly commentaries.

Below are notes on a few of the poems:

9   There is an old legend that the cross was made of an apple tree directly descended from the tree that tempted Adam and Eve.

14   Jesus is the speaker.

19   The speaker is one of the practical men who sentenced Jesus to death.

21   This poem is a dramatic monologue by a retired Roman soldier. He is biased against the Jews and not interested in the legal and moral complexities of the trial and execution of Jesus.

23   This poem is frankly based on a long-standing mistranslation of verse 20. The Hebrew is: "Deliver . . . my only one from the power of the dog," and is equivalent to "Deliver . . . my very self from the power of the dog." But I yielded to the poetic impetus of the familiar King James words.

24   Here again I have clung to an older wording for poetic reasons. "Unicorns" is soberly and correctly translated "wild oxen" in the RSV. Folklore takes the unicorn as a symbol of purity; in my poem the purity is of a pallid, somewhat self-righteous kind. The lion (for my present purposes) symbolizes the carnal temptations and sins. Thus the poem deals with carnal sins and their more perilous cousins, the spiritual sins.

25 One of the Old Testament names for God is Yahweh (Jehovah), a word with four consonants (Tetragrammaton). The Hebrews, out of reverence, hesitated to speak the holy name. ' IXΘύς (*ichthys*) is the Greek word for fish. The five letters form the initial letters of a Greek phrase, *Iēsous Christos theou hyios sōtēr*—Jesus Christ, Son of God, Savior. For this reason, as well as other powerful reasons of symbolism, the fish is a frequent symbol for Christ. The poem is written in the form of a sermon.

27 An angel is talking to another angel.

28 My family and I have a summer cottage at a small lake in northern Vermont. The poem describes a Communion service in the living room. The idea I wish to suggest is that, at every act of worship, there are more people present than the visible ones. The whole Church Triumphant participates.

30 Judas is speaking.

37 In my mind, I have associated verse 29 of the psalm with the assertion in the Apostles' Creed, "He descended into hell." ("Hell" in the Creed means "place of departed spirits.")

38 The text of verse 29 is somewhat corrupt. "None can keep alive his own soul" is probably not the original reading. I have, however, retained it because it served as an evocative quotation for a poem.

40 Addressed to any unborn child.

A technical note for those interested in such matters:
I once asked my good friend, Professor John G. Hocking,

of the mathematics department at Michigan State University, whether there was any way the mathematics of probability could be utilized to create poetic forms that would have an overall feeling of unity but great variation within the unity. After considerable experimentation—during the course of which he composed several interesting poems—he suggested the use of dice to determine the rhyme scheme, line length, and the occurrence of unrhymed lines. Poem 7, which reads rather like one of the so-called "Cowleyan odes" of the seventeenth century, was the result of an experiment I made at his suggestion. I modified the mathematical patterns in only a few places, mainly by omitting a couple of lines of verse called for by the dice. Naturally, I had to determine for myself when to leave a particular sequence of rhymes and begin a new one.

I suppose this experiment has some bearing on the persistent question of the relation between form and content in poetry and the other arts, but I leave the reader to draw his own conclusions.

other books in the **Wheaton Literary Series:**

The Achievement of C. S. Lewis, by Thomas Howard. "Written with Lewis's own passionate power with words."—*Peter Kreeft.* Paper, 196 pages

Adam, by David Bolt. An imaginative retelling of the Genesis 1-3 narrative. "I think it splendid."—*C. S. Lewis.* Cloth, 143 pages

Creation in Christ: Unspoken Sermons, by George MacDonald, edited by Rolland Hein. Devotional essays revealing a deeply moving understanding of holiness and man's relationship to God. Paper, 342 pages

Geometries of Light, poems by Eugene Warren. "He shows how abundantly love has poured Itself into our 'seed-filled light' and 'night-locked flesh.' "—*Robert Siegel.* Paper, 108 pages

A Guide Through Narnia, by Martha C. Sammons. A detailed study of Lewis and his Chronicles of Narnia, with map, chronology and index of names and places. Paper, 165 pages

Images of Salvation in the Fiction of C. S. Lewis, by Clyde S. Kilby. Explores the Christian meaning in Lewis's juvenile and adult fiction. Cloth, 140 pages

Life Essential: The Hope of the Gospel, by George MacDonald, edited by Rolland Hein. "A book for those who hunger after righteousness."—*Corbin S. Carnell.* Paper, 102 pages

Listen to the Green, poems by Luci Shaw. Poems that see through nature and human nature to God. Illustrated with photographs. Paper, 93 pages

The Miracles of Our Lord, by George MacDonald, edited by Rolland Hein. "A better set of meditations on the miracles of Christ would be hard to find."—*Walter Elwell.* Paper, 170 pages

The Secret Trees, poems by Luci Shaw. "These are the real thing, true poems . . . they work by magic."—*Calvin Linton.* Cloth, 79 pages

The Sighting, poems by Luci Shaw. "Few poets in our day can speak of incarnational reality with the eloquence of Luci Shaw."—Harold Fickett. Paper, illustrated with photographs, 96 pages

Tolkien and The Silmarillion, by Clyde S. Kilby. A fascinating view of Tolkien as a scholar, writer, creator and Christian, based on Kilby's close association during the collation of The Silmarillion. Cloth, 89 pages

Walking on Water: Reflections on Faith & Art, by Madeleine L'Engle. Shows us the impact of the Word on words and ourselves as co-creators with God. Cloth, 198 pages

The Weather of the Heart, poems by Madeleine L'Engle. "Read her poetry and be chastened and filled with joy."—*Thomas Howard.* Cloth, 96 pages

The World of George MacDonald: Selections from His Works of Fiction, edited by Rolland Hein. "A treasure of a book—one to be read and re-read."—*Frank E. Gaebelein.* Paper, 199 pages

Available from your local bookstore, or from
HAROLD SHAW PUBLISHERS, Box 567, Wheaton, Ill. 60187